All You Want

Med

Vikas Malkani

Reprint 2001

New Dawn

NEW DAWN
An imprint of Sterling Publishers (P) Ltd.
L-10, Green Park Extension, New Delhi-110016
Ph.: 6191784, 6191785, 6191023 Fax: 91-11-6190028
E-mail: ghai@nde.vsnl.net.in
Internet: http://www.sterlingpublishers.com

All You Wanted to Know About - Meditation
©2000, Sterling Publishers Private Limited
ISBN 81 207 2347 3
Reprint 2001

Published by Sterling Publishers Pvt. Ltd., New Delhi-110016.
Lasertypeset by Vikas Compographics, New Delhi-110029.
Printed at Shagun Offset, New Delhi-110029.

Contents

3

Introduction

In every culture and society, all over the world, people are educated in the skills needed to function and survive in that culture — how to talk, think, work, and investigate the objects and experiences of the external world. We learn sciences such as biology, ecology, and chemistry in order to understand the world we live in, but no one teaches us how to understand or attend to our own inner dimensions, neither in any school nor in any college or university. We merely learn to assimilate the goals, fashions, and values of our society, without really knowing ourselves. This leaves us ignorant of ourselves and dependent on the advice and suggestions of others.

Meditation is a very different, subtle, and precise approach; it is a simple technique of learning to pay attention to and understand all the various levels of our selves — the body, the breathing process, the aspects of stress. As time progresses, you may find that you enjoy the positive results from meditation —

increased joyfulness, clarity, and awareness — as much as you enjoy the relief of the physical, nervous, and mental symptoms of stress. Meditation will certainly help you in locating your inner self — the real you.

What is Meditation?

Etymologically, the root of the word, "meditation" is similar to the root word for "medical" or "medicate," and the root of all these words implies a sense of "attending to" or "paying attention to" something. In meditation, you pay attention to those dimensions of yourself that are seldom observed or known—that is, your own inner levels, lying deep within you. These deeper levels are more profound than the processes of thinking, analyzing, day-dreaming, or experiencing emotions or memories.

Meditation involves a type of "inner attention" that is quiet, concentrated, and at the same time, relaxed. There is nothing strenuous or difficult about creating this "inner attention", in fact, meditation is a process that is restful and relaxing for the mind. In the beginning, the greatest difficulty is that the mind has never been trained to create this inner attention. Once that is accomplished the rest becomes easy.

You will find that you do not need to do anything different or demanding physically, that your meditation does not require you to adopt any strange or foreign habits, and that you do not have to meditate for long or extended periods of time in order to progress and observe the benefits. You will enjoy the practice of meditation! Your body will be more relaxed, your mind will become more creative and focused, and you may even notice significant improvements in your health and relationships!

Therapeutic Properties of Meditation

Meditation is therapeutic from the very beginning; it helps relax the tension of the gross and subtle muscles and the autonomous nervous system, and it provides freedom from mental stress. A person in meditation attains a tranquil mind, and this helps the immune system by limiting its reaction to stress and strain. You will find that even a few days' sincere efforts will help you to control your appetite and severe reactions like anger to a certain degree. Meditation will also decrease the need for sleep and energize the body and mind.

Those who are writers, poets, and thinkers often express interest in the process of becoming creative and using their intuition, the finest and most evolved of all aspects of knowledge. Meditation is a systematic way of using this aspect of human brilliance in our daily life.

Meditation also has an important influence on health. In the modern world, most diseases can be classified to some degree as psychosomatic — having their origins in, or being influenced by the human mind, thoughts, and emotions. Recently, scientists have begun to recognize that these diseases cannot really be "cured" merely by the conventional methods of orthodox medicine or psychotherapy alone, because if the disease originates in the mind or is caused due to various emotional reactions, how can external therapy alone restore your health? If you rely only on external remedies, and do not seek to understand your own mind and emotions, you may merely become dependent on a therapist or a physician for help. In contrast, the process of meditation makes people self-reliant, and helps them to attain the inner strength necessary to deal more effectively with all the problems in life.

Meditation as a Process

In the process of meditation, we ask the mind to let go of its tendencies to think, analyze, remember, solve problems, and focus on the events of the past or on the expectations of the future. We help the mind to slow down its rapid series of thoughts and feelings, and to replace that mental activity with an inner awareness and attention.

Thus, meditation is not 'thinking about' problems or analyzing a situation. It is not fantasizing or day-dreaming or merely letting the mind wander aimlessly. Meditation is not having an internal conversation or argument with yourself or intensifying the thinking process. Meditation is simply a quiet, effortless, one-point focus of attention and awareness.

While meditating, we try to let go of all the mental distractions, preoccupations, and the fleeting thoughts and associations of our normal waking experience. We do this, not by trying to make the mind empty, which is impossible, but instead, by allowing the mind to focus on one subtle element or object, which leads the attention further inward. By giving the mind one internal focus of attention, we help it to refrain from other stressful mental processes, such as worrying, planning, thinking, and reasoning.

Sounds which are used to help in mental concentration during meditation are called *mantras,* and they have very powerful effects on the mental level.

A mantra may be a word, a phrase, a set of sounds or simply a syllable. Concentrating on a mantra helps the students to ignore their useless, distracting mental tensions, and proceed into the depths of their inner selves. Many different kinds of mantras are used throughout the world, including mantras such as *Om, Amen,* and *Shalom,* and they all have the similar goal of helping you focus your mind.

In all the great spiritual traditions of the world, whether ancient or modern, there is some system of pronouncing such a syllable, sound or set of words that act like a mantra. This is a profound and great science, and those who are competent in this science can lead students on the same path. The preliminary practices by aspirants are simple and easy, but when one begins to deal with the mind, the prescription of an appropriate mantra can be seen to be very effective and powerful.

The meditative texts and scriptures speak extensively on this subject. Patanjali, the codifier of the 'yoga' science, says that the mantra becomes a representative of the innermost source of consciousness. Therefore, it becomes a leader and even a bridge between the mortal and immortal parts of life. When the body, breath, and conscious mind separate from the unconscious mind and the individual soul, the conscious effort of having remembered such a mantra goes on creating impressions in the unconscious. These impressions are powerful motivators, which help the aspirant during the period of transition which we call death, and then it becomes easier for him or her to make the unknown voyage.

Just as there are many different paths one could take to climb a mountain, there are a variety of seemingly "different" meditation practices or techniques. Yet all have the same goal— achieving a state of inner concentration, calmness, and serenity. Any practice that helps you to achieve this is beneficial. Many valid techniques exist, so there is really no difference between one type of authentic meditation and another, as long as they help you attain this inner stillness and focus.

If we observe life carefully, we realise that right from our childhood, we have only been trained and educated in how to examine and verify things in the external world, and that no one has actually taught us how to look within, find within, and verify within. Therefore, the human being remains a stranger to himself or herself, while trying to establish various sorts of relationships in the external world. That is why none of these relationships really seem to work successfully, and confusion and disappointments prevail.

Very little of the mind is cultivated by our formal

educational system. The part of the mind that dreams and sleeps, the vast realm of the unconscious, which is the reservoir of all our experiences, remains unknown and undisciplined; it is not subjected to any control. It is true that "the whole of the body is in the mind, but the whole of the mind is not in the body." There is no other method of truly developing control over the totality of the mind, except through the practice of meditation.

We are taught how to move and behave in the external world, but we are never taught how to be still and examine what is within ourselves. At the same time, learning to be still and calm should not be made a ceremony or a part of any religion; it is a universal requirement of the human body. When one learns to sit still, he or she attains a kind of joy that is inexplicable. The highest of all joys that can ever be attained or experienced by a human being is attained through meditation. All the other joys in the world are transient and momentary, but the joy of meditation is immense and everlasting. This is not an exaggeration, but a simple fact, a truth that is supported by a long line of great sages, both those who renounced the world and attained the Truth, and those who attained the Truth without renouncing the world.

The mind has a tendency to wander into the "grooves" of its old habit patterns, and then it imagines those experiences in the future. The mind does not really know how to be in the present, here and now. Only meditation teaches us to fully experience the now, which is a part of the eternal. When, with the help of meditative techniques, the mind is focused at a point, it attains the power of penetrating into the deeper levels of one's being. Then, the mind does not create any distractions or deviations; it fully attains the power of concentration, which is a prerequisite for meditation.

To begin this path, understand clearly what meditation is, select a practice that is comfortable for you, and do it consistently and regularly for some time, every day, at the same time , if possible. In the modern world, however, students tend to become impatient easily and they practise only for a brief period of time before they finally give up, concluding that there is no value or authenticity in the technique. This is like a child who plants a tulip bulb and is frustrated because he sees no flowers in a week! You will definitely experience progress if you meditate regularly.

At first, you may see the progress in terms of immediate physical relaxation and calmness. Later, you may notice other, more subtle, benefits. Some of the most important benefits of meditation make themselves known gradually over a period of time, and are not dramatic or easily observed. Persist in your meditation and you will notice progress.

Meditation is not Contemplation or Thinking

Contemplation, especially the contemplation of inspiring concepts or ideals—such as truth, peace, and love—can be very helpful, although it is distinct and different from the process of meditation. While contemplating, you engage your mind in inquiring into this concept, and take into consideration the meaning and value of the concept.

In the system of meditation, contemplation is considered a separate practice, one that can be very useful at times. When you engage yourself in meditation, you do not ask the mind to think or contemplate on any concept: instead, you allow it to go beyond this level of mental activity.

**Meditation is not
Hypnosis or Auto-suggestion**
In hypnosis, a suggestion is made to the mind, either by another person or by your own self. Such a suggestion may take the form of, "You are feeling sleepy (or

relaxed)." Thus in hypnosis there is an attempt to program, manipulate or control the content of the mind to make it believe a certain fact, or think in an ordered, particular way. Sometimes, such powerful suggestions can be very useful. Unfortunately, negative suggestions have negative effects on us and our health.

In meditation, you do not make any attempts to give the mind a direct suggestion or to control the mind. You simply observe and let the mind become quiet and calm, allowing your mantra to lead you deeper within, exploring and experiencing the deeper levels of your being.

Meditation is not a Religion

Meditation is not some strange or foreign practice that requires you to change your beliefs, your culture or your religion. Meditation is not a religion at all; rather, it is a very practical, scientific, and systematic technique for knowing yourself at all levels. Meditation does not "belong to" any culture or religion of the world.

Religion teaches people what to believe in, but meditation teaches you to experience directly for yourself. There is no conflict between these two techniques. Worship is a part of the religious system, as is prayer, which is a dialogue with the divine principle. Certainly, you can be both a religious person who prays, and a meditator who uses the techniques of meditation, but it is not necessary to have an orthodox religion, to meditate. Meditation should be practised as a pure technique, in a systematic, orderly way.

Before we begin to meditate, we should have some faith in the process by which meditation helps us in achieving those much desired results.

In order to meditate, we will need to learn:

- How to relax the body.

- How to sit in a comfortable, steady position for meditation.

- How to make our breathing process serene.

- How to witness the objects travelling in the train of the mind.

- How to inspect the quality of thoughts, and learn to promote or strengthen those which are positive and helpful in our growth.

- How to prevent ourselves from being disturbed in any situation, whether we judge it as good or bad.

If you practise meditation with a clear understanding of what it is, and with the appropriate techniques and attitudes, you will find it refreshing and energizing.

Meditate to Rejuvenate

Meditation is the best time investment you can make. If you believe that health is wealth, then the time you set aside every day for your meditation session will make you a rich person. Many studies have shown that meditation significantly improves our health level. The stress released and the energy produced when we meditate, activate the body's own healing forces.

All healing comes from within. Drugs merely suppress the symptoms and often do nothing to remove the cause of the problem. In fact, in most cases drugs produce harmful side effects, thereby aggravating the situation. Meditation is an excellent complement to conventional medicine or surgery. Patients who meditate heal themselves faster.

Theoretically, we should wake up every morning feeling fresh and alive, ready to tackle whatever the day has in store for us. But this is not the case always. The problem is, we do not always sleep peacefully, or long enough. Physical discomfort, mental worries or just not feeling relaxed are obstacles to a good sleep that can lead to rest and relaxation. This is where meditation comes to the rescue. By giving our nervous system an additional period of deep rest twice a day, we can compensate for a bad night's sleep, so that we feel good and have a productive day.

Studies show that during both sleep and meditation, our metabolic rate slows down. The metabolic rate refers to how quickly the body uses oxygen to "burn up" the nutrients from the food we consume, to produce energy. A low metabolic rate indicates that the body is not using up much oxygen and is in a more restful state. The metabolic rate is considered a good indicator of how relaxed the body is. The remarkable thing is that meditation produces a lower metabolic rate than sleep. During sleep, it takes four or five hours to produce an eight per cent drop in metabolic rate, while during a thirty minute meditation, we achieve a drop between ten per cent and twenty per cent. This means meditation produces a much deeper state of rest than sleep, and in a much shorter time. In addition, alpha waves are produced by the brain during meditation, which also signifies a deep state of rest. Alpha waves are not usually produced during sleep.

However, this does not mean that you do not need to sleep, for sleep has many other functions besides producing rest, and is essential for our well-being and overall mental balance. When the nervous system is rested by meditation, our brain works at peak efficiency. This means we display more intelligence, more creativity and more feelings. This is especially significant, since happiness and success depend to a large extent on these three factors. Deep rest also makes us feel good, since it relaxes the nervous system and allows it to be recharged with energy. The deep rest produced by meditation is mainly due to the reduction in thought when we meditate. Thoughts actually produce waves which are registered in the brain as electrical activity. If our thoughts are excessive (and in most of us they are), then this electrical activity becomes excessive and is a disturbance to the brain. We feel this unpleasantness and tension in the mind, and call it stress. Meditation greatly reduces the amount of electrical activity in the brain. The brain becomes calm, and we can feel this in the mind as a pleasant peacefulness. In meditation, the brain is given a rest, which allows it to recuperate and rejuvenate.

Deep Rest Leads to Rejuvenation

Deep rest activates the body's healing forces, allowing rejuvenation of the body to occur. Once the metabolic rate slows down, the body then directs some of its energy for healing and rejuvenation. We become healthier as a result of meditation. Minor and sometimes major health disorders disappear, and we start to look and feel younger. Disease is actually a very apt word, for it implies not being at ease (dis...ease).

Not only the body, but the mind also feels rejuvenated. For probably the first time in your life, your mind, through meditation, gets a rest during the day. Body and mind have in-built abilities to rejuvenate — they just need the right conditions. Meditation provides you the key to both of these.

Meditation Leads to Rejuvenation

- Meditation promises a deeper rest than sleep, in a much shorter time. This causes our brain to work at peak efficiency: we display more intelligence, creativity and feeling. It also makes us feel good, since deep rest relaxes the nervous system and recharges it with energy.

- Deep rest reactivates the body's healing forces, allowing rejuvenation of the body and mind to occur.

Health Benefits of Meditation

The stress released as a result of meditation brings about some very important health benefits.

Reduced Blood Pressure
The release of stress relaxes our muscles and the muscular walls of our blood vessels. This means more blood is pumped through the vessels, and there is less resistance to the overall flow, which in turn means low blood pressure. In contrast, high blood pressure is

recognised as a major factor in producing heart diseases and heart attacks.

In an American study on stress management, thirty-five people with an average systolic blood pressure of 146 were placed under observation. After just a few weeks of meditation, their blood pressure had dropped to 137. A drop of almost 10 points is very significant, lowering the blood pressure from the borderline high range to the normal range. This is far better than taking drugs, which have side effects and do nothing to tackle the cause of the problem. Addressing only the effect of the problem and not the cause is never a long term solution.

Improved Sleep

When we are meditating regularly, we tend to fall asleep quicker, and our sleep is deeper. This means we get more and better quality sleep. As a result, we wake up feeling more fresh and alive than before. We also feel more energetic and calm throughout the day.

Increased Circulation to All Organs and Glands

Relaxed blood vessels allow increased blood flow to all the parts of the body. Increased blood flow to the brain means we feel more fresh and can think more clearly. It also helps us to prevent strokes. Increased blood flow to the digestive system means it will function better, and we will digest and assimilate food better.

Balances the two Hemispheres of the Brain

Studies show that meditation has a balancing and harmonizing effect on the right and left hemispheres of the brain. Our left hemisphere is responsible for thinking. It is the logical, analytical side of the brain.

The right side is responsible for feelings. Due to the pace and nature of modern life, many of us tend to operate more from the left hemisphere. We think too much and analyse too much, at the expense of our feelings.

Meditation allows us to have the right balance of logical, analytical thought and emotional feelings.

Helps Asthma

A clinical research conducted by Ron Honsberger and Archie F. Wilson in the USA reported that asthmatic patients showed improvement in their asthma after taking to meditation. Ninety-four per cent of the group showed less air passage resistance, fifty-five per cent showed improvement as reported by their personal physicians; and seventy-four per cent stated that they themselves felt an improvement.

Stimulates Hormonal Activity

Meditation stimulates our glands to produce more hormones. Studies show that hormone levels in meditators are similar to those in people up to ten years younger than the meditator. This is one of the reasons why meditators look and feel younger. At the same time, meditation causes a reduction in the production of our stress hormones - adrenaline and noradrenaline.

Assists Health Problems

Up to seventy per cent of health problems are psychosomatic, that is, they have a mental origin, so it is easy to understand how a reduction in stress due to meditation can help cure many of these disorders.

Reversal of Ageing

Biomechanical age measures how old a person is physiologically. As a group, long-term meditators who had been practising meditation for more than five years, were physiologically twelve years younger than their chronological age, as measured by reduction of blood pressure, and better near-point vision and auditory discrimination. Short-term meditators were physiologically five years younger than their chronological age. The study, conducted in the United States, took into consideration the effects of diet and exercise.

Alert yet at Rest
In their electroencephalographic studies, the French team comprising Jean-Paul Banquet and Maurice

Sailhan reported that, during meditation, a greater proportion of alpha waves were produced, compared to delta waves. This indicates a heightened level of wakefulness. In addition, the ratio of beta waves to alpha waves was reduced, indicating a more relaxed state. It is this unique combination of deep relaxation and increased alertness that differentiates meditation from other relaxation techniques and sleep. It is referred to as the meditative state of consciousness or the super-conscious state. It indicates the emergence of the higher consciousness.

The findings of several studies published in various science journals show that meditation increases the EEG index of restful alertness — increases slow, alpha frequency power in the frontal cortex. This change in the EEG indicates a relaxed state of wakefulness during meditation, and an ordered state of brain functioning, both of which are ideal for dynamic activity.

Meditation Optimises
Brain Function

Reports published in the International Journal of Neuroscience claim that higher levels of EEG coherence, measured during the practice of meditation, are significantly correlated with increased fluency of verbal creativity, increased efficiency in learning new concepts, more principled moral reasoning, higher verbal IQ, decreased neuroticism, clearer experiences of trans-cendental consciousness and increased neurological efficiency.

Meditation Decreases the Dependency on Drugs

A study on the effect of meditation on drug use was undertaken in the United States by Dr. R. K. Wallace, Dr. H. Benson and Associates. Two questionnaires were sent to almost two thousand people who were experienced meditators. About eighteen hundred people responded. The subjects were asked to record their drug-use habits before and after starting meditation.

In the six-month period prior to starting meditation, seventy-eight per cent had used either marijuana and hashish or both, and twenty-eight per cent of this group were heavy users (once a day or more). After six months of regular meditation, only thirty-seven per cent continued to use marijuana — that is, a forty per cent drop. After 21 months of meditation, only twelve per cent continued to use marijuana — a sixty-six per cent drop. Of those who still took drugs, only one was a heavy user.

Meditation was even more successful with LSD users. After twenty-two months of meditation, ninety-seven per cent of LSD users had given it up.

There was also a high rate of success with heavy narcotics including heroin, opium, morphine and cocaine. Before meditation, seventeen per cent used these drugs, and after a twenty-two to twenty-three month period of meditation, only one per cent continued to use them.

When questioned why the meditators gave up drugs, the general response was that they enjoyed the profound feelings from meditation more than the feelings aroused by drugs.

Changes in Lifestyle .

As meditation connects you to your Real or Natural Self, you gradually feel an increasing desire to live more in harmony with nature. You will also gravitate towards a simpler lifestyle without extra or unnecessary burdens. You will desire more natural things such as nourishing food, fresh air and exercise. If you smoke or drink alcohol excessively, your taste for these vices will diminish. You will stop overeating.

Meditation causes your innate intelligence and life force to manifest itself more strongly. This results in an urge to live more in accordance with nature's laws. Since your mind is less cluttered with unnecessary thoughts, you can focus on your goals in a better way.

Meditation has a powerful effect on relationships of all kinds. Our relationships with other people also improve. We cease to worry about other people hurting us. In any case, we tend to attract people who can contribute to our lives in many ways.

When our mind calms down and our higher consciousness starts expressing itself, we tend to become less subjective and more objective.

Medical Proof that Meditation Releases Stress

Electrical activity of the brain can be measured by an electro-encephalogram. Wires are connected from this instrument to the scalp and forehead.

In a study done by Dr. A. Kasamatsu and Dr. Hirai of the University of Tokyo, it was found that when Zen monks meditated, they produced a predominance of alpha waves. In addition, the alpha waves increased in amplitude and regularity during meditation. This same effect was found by researchers in India when they did studies on Yogis during meditation.

This predominance of alpha waves is associated with a state of deep relaxation and a feeling of well-being. It verifies that meditation is extremely effective in releasing stress.

Meditation Creates Restful Awareness

Once you understand stress and know the various ways of releasing it, you start to look after your health. When you relax, the easy feeling makes you feel good for a while and then life takes over. Again you experience mood swings, fear, anxiety and depression. You then realise you have not yet emptied your load of regrets and grudges.

Now comes the time for the Ultimate Life Maintenance programme. You need to form the habit of restful awareness, and this is achieved through meditation.

Meditation is your way into a higher level of consciousness where you can calmly and correctly assess the various aspects of your life. Only after you have overcome and transcended your inner conflicts caused out of excessive desires, ego-tripping, long-standing grudges, low self-esteem and the need to control other people's lives, will your life become truly stable and enjoyable.

The habit of meditation is worth developing and results in a life of alert and joyful tranquillity.

Here are some facts about meditation. Meditation has been a part of all religions, since religion began. It does not involve severe concentration. We do not meditate for the purpose of producing any extraordinary powers. If they do occur, they are considered merely a side effect. Withdrawing from the mainstream of life is just the opposite of what we are trying to achieve when we meditate. By bringing out our full potential, meditation allows us to enjoy life to the fullest. We do not have to retreat to the caves for our sessions - the same results can be reaped even if we are to meditate in the comfort of our homes. Once the habit is developed, meditation is simple and effortless.

Anyone can meditate. Meditation is a simple, natural and effortless technique to quieten down and pacify the mind, making us experience an inner peace and tranquillity that leads us to our true inner selves.

Meditation is simple because it works in harmony with your true nature or your higher consciousness. The state of total health, peace and happiness is already there: all you have to do is use a technique to arrive at it. Meditation is a very powerful, time-efficient and safe way of doing this. It is a time-honoured technique, having proven itself for thousands of years.

Postures for Meditation

Meditation is a simple technique that almost everyone can enjoy. To meditate, you simply sit quietly and comfortably in a relaxed and steady position. You still the body, make the breathing process serene, and then allow the mind to become quiet and focused.

These three stages are a movement from the most external, physical level to the most subtle level.

Sitting Postures for Meditation

The requirements for a good meditation posture are that it be still, steady, relaxed, and comfortable. If the body moves, sways, twitches or aches, it will distract you from meditation. Some people have the misconception that to meditate, you must sit in a complicated, crosslegged position called the "lotus pose." Fortunately, this is not true; there is actually only one important prerequisite for a good meditation posture, and that is, it must allow you to keep the head, neck, and trunk of the body aligned so that you can breathe freely and diaphragmatically.

Position of the Head, Neck, and Trunk

In all the meditative postures, the head and neck should be centred, so that the neck is not twisted or turned to either side, nor is the head held too forward. The head should be supported by the neck and held directly over the shoulders without creating any tension in the neck or shoulders. Face forward, with your eyes gently closed. Simply allow the eyes to close and do not create any pressure on the eyes. Some people have unfortunately been told to try to force their gaze upwards to a specific point in their forehead. This position creates strain and tension in the eyes and may even produce a headache. There are some yogic practices that involve specific gazes, but they are not used during meditation. Simply let all the facial muscles relax. The mouth should also be gently closed, without any tension in the jaw. All breathing is done through the nostrils.

Position of the Shoulders, Arms, and Hands

In all the meditative positions, your shoulders and arms are relaxed and allowed to rest gently on the knees, as you will see in the illustrations. Your arms should be so completely relaxed, that if someone were to pick up your hand, your arm would be limp. You can gently join the thumb and index fingers in a position called the "finger lock." This *mudra* or gesture creates a circle, which you may think of, symbolically, as a small circuit that recycles energy within, rather than extending your energy outward.

Sitting Positions for Meditation
There are many positions that allow you to sit comfortably, keeping the

spine aligned, without twisting your legs or creating any discomfort. In fact, the arms and legs are not really important in meditation. What is important is that the spine be correctly aligned. The easiest way to accomplish this is a posture called *Maitri asana* or Friendship Pose (See Figure 1).

Friendship pose (Maitri asana)
In *Maitri asana*, you sit comfortably on a chair or a bench, with your feet flat on the floor and your hands resting on your lap. *Maitri asana* can be used by anyone, even those who are not very flexible or comfortable

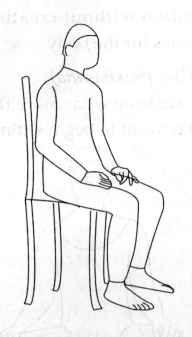

Figure 1: Friendship Pose (*Maitri asana*)

sitting on the floor. This posture
allows you to begin the process of

meditation without creating any difficulties for the body.

Easy Pose (Sukhasana)

If you are somewhat more flexible, you may want to begin sitting in an

Figure 2: Easy Pose (*Sukhasana*)

alternative position, called the Easy Pose or *Sukhasana* (Figure 2). In the Easy Pose, you sit in a simple, cross-legged position on the floor or a platform. As you can see in the illustration, in Easy Pose, the feet are placed on the floor under the opposite knees, and the knees rest gently on the opposite feet. Place a folded blanket underneath yourself, so that your knees or ankles do not receive too much pressure. Your meditation seat should be firm, but neither too hard nor shaky. The seat should not be so high that it disturbs your body position.

If your legs are less flexible or your thigh muscles are tight, you may find that your knees remain fairly off the floor. Several warm-up stretching postures will be beneficial in developing greater flexibility, thereby increasing your comfort. Whatever position you select, practise it regularly and avoid frequent attempts at new postures — if you work regularly on one sitting posture, it will become comfortable and steady over a period of time.

The Auspicious Pose (Swastikasana)

The Auspicious Pose, *Swastikasana* (Figure 3) offers several advantages

Figure 3: Auspicious Pose (*Swastikasana*)

to those who can sit in this posture
comfortably. If your legs are fairly
flexible, you may actually find it
more comfortable than the Easy
Pose, for longer periods of

meditation. Since the position has a wider foundation, it distributes the body weight more directly on the floor, and is somewhat steadier and less likely to lead to swaying or other bodily movements.

In *Swastikasana,* the knees rest directly on the floor, rather than on the feet. One advantage of this posture, for some students, is that the ankle bones also receive less weight or pressure.

To develop the Auspicious Pose *(Swastikasana)*, you begin by sitting comfortably on your meditation seat, and then you bend the left leg at the knee and place the left foot alongside the right thigh. The sole or the bottom of the left foot may be flat against the inside of the right thigh. Next, the right knee is bent, and the right foot is placed gently on the left calf, with the bottom of the foot against the thigh. The upper surface of the right foot is gently placed between the thigh and the back of the left calf, tucking in the toes. Finally, with your hand, you gently bring the toes of your left foot up between the right thigh and calf, so that the big toe is now visible. This creates a very symmetrical and stable posture, which is very effective for meditation. While the above description may sound complicated, you will find that if you follow the directions, it is not difficult.

Finding Your Own Comfortable Position

For beginners, the Auspicious Pose may not be comfortable initially because they lack flexibility in their legs. You can certainly sit in any individual variation of a cross-legged pose that allows you to be steady and keep the body still without jerkiness or swaying, or you may begin with *Maitri asana*. The point to be noted is: it is more important to keep the head, neck, and trunk correctly positioned, so that the spine is aligned, than to put your legs in some particular position.

Problems with Back Muscles

Modern people tend to have poor posture because of the bad habits that they have developed for walking and sitting. Due to this, the muscles that are meant to support the spinal column remain underdeveloped, and the spine tends to curve with age, distorting the body. When you first begin sitting in meditation, you may notice that your back muscles are weak and that after a few minutes of sitting, you tend to slump forward.

Actually, this problem can be solved in very little time if you begin to pay attention to your posture throughout the day while sitting, standing and walking. Adjust your posture when you notice that you are slumping. In this way, the back muscles will begin to do their job appropriately.

Some students with poor posture ask if they can do their meditation leaning back against a wall for support. In the beginning, you can do this to develop a correctly aligned posture or to check your alignment, although it is not good to remain dependent on such support. From the beginning, it is best to work consciously and attentively with your posture. Ask a friend to check, or examine your posture while watching sideways in a mirror. If the spinal column is correctly aligned, you will not feel the knobs of the spinal vertebrae jutting out while you run your hand up your back.

Suggestions for Making Sitting Positions More Comfortable

Most people find it easier to sit on the floor if they use a folded blanket to provide a padding for the entire area, or use a thick cushion or pillow under the buttocks and hips alone, supporting that part of the body which is three to four inches off the floor. Elevating the buttocks in this manner seems to relieve much of the pressure on the hip joints and knees, and you may be amazed to see the difference it makes. Using a thick cushion under your buttocks will also make it easier to keep your spine correctly aligned.

As you become more flexible and comfortable, you may find that you can use a thinner cushion and eventually sit flat on the floor. However, it is important to keep the spine aligned and not allow it to curve over, disturbing your posture. At first, some people find it difficult to maintain this alignment without a thick cushion. Be patient in developing your sitting posture; you will find that your body gradually becomes more flexible and that you can sit for longer periods more comfortably.

Stretching exercises and Hatha yoga asanas can be very beneficial in helping you to make the body more flexible and comfortable in meditation.

Breathing Exercises

There are many pranayama (breathing) exercises. The following exercises are very important for beginners.

The Complete Breath
The complete breath helps expand the capacity of the lungs, and is excellent as a physical and mental energizing exercise. If possible, practise the exercise in front of an open window or out of doors.

While doing the exercise it may be helpful to imagine yourself as a glass of water being emptied and filled. When the water is poured out, the glass empties from the top to the bottom. When the water is poured in, the glass fills from the bottom to the top.

Technique

Assume a simple and relaxed standing posture:

Try inhaling, filling the lower lungs first, then the middle lungs, and then the upper lungs; simultaneously, raise the arms until they are overhead, with hands joined together in a prayer position.

Then exhale, emptying the upper lungs first, then the middle lungs, and then the lower lungs; simultaneously, lower the arms back to the side.

Repeat the exercise two to five more times.

Diaphragmatic Breathing

Although breathing is one of the most vital functions, it is little understood and often done improperly. Most people breathe shallowly and haphazardly, going against the natural rhythmic movement of the body's respiratory system. Diaphragmatic breathing,

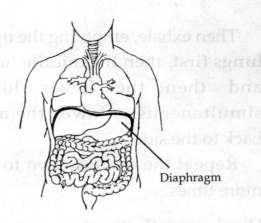

Diaphragm

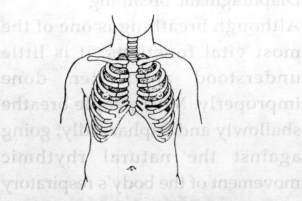

Location of the diaphragm in relation to the ribs
and internal organs.

on the other hand, promotes a natural, even breath movement that strengthens the nervous system and relaxes the body. The importance of deep, even breathing in meditation cannot be overemphasised.

Respiration is normally, of either of the two types, or a combination of both: chest or abdominal. Chest breathing or shallow breathing is characterised by an outward movement of the upper chest. Deep abdominal breathing is characterised by an outward movement of the abdominal wall due to the contraction and descent of the diaphragm. Practitioners of yoga recognise a third type of breathing, known as diaphragmatic breathing, which focuses attention on the diaphragm in the lower rib cage. It is this method of breathing that is practised during the asana. Diaphragmatic breathing should not be confused with abdominal or belly breathing, which is also sometimes referred to as deep diaphragmatic breathing.

The principal muscle of diaphragmatic breathing — the diaphragm— is a strong, horizontal, dome-shaped muscle. It divides the thoracic cavity, which contains the heart and lungs, from the abdominal cavity, which contains the organs of digestion, reproduction, and excretion. The diaphragm is located approximately at mid-chest, in its relaxed or dome-shaped state.

During inhalation, the diaphragm contracts and flattens; it gets pushed downwards, causing the upper abdominal muscles to relax and extend slightly, and the lower "floating" ribs to flare slightly outward. In this position the lungs expand, creating a partial vacuum, which draws air into the chest cavity. During exhalation, the diaphragm relaxes and returns to its dome-shaped position. During this upward movement, the upper abdominal muscles contract, and the carbon dioxide is forced from the lungs.

Diaphragmatic breathing has three important effects on the body:

- In diaphragmatic breathing, unlike shallow breathing, the lungs are filled completely, providing the body with sufficient oxygen.

- Diaphragmatic breathing forces out the waste products of the respiratory process and carbon dioxide, from the lungs. When breathing shallowly, some amount of carbon dioxide may remain trapped in the lungs, thereby causing fatigue and nervousness.

- The up and down motion of the diaphragm gently massages the abdominal organs; this increases circulation to these organs and thus aids in their functioning.

In diaphragmatic breathing, a very minimal effort is used to receive a large amount of air; thus, it is the most efficient method of breathing.

Technique

Lie on the back keeping the feet apart at a comfortable distance. Gently close the eyes and place one hand on the upper abdomen and the other on the chest.

Inhale and exhale through the nostrils slowly, smoothly, and evenly, with no noise, jerks, or pauses in the breath. While inhaling, be aware of the upper abdominal muscles expanding and the lower ribs flaring out slightly. There should be little or no movement of the chest.

Practise this method of deep breathing for three to five minutes daily until you clearly understand the movement of the diaphragm and the upper abdominal muscles. The body is designed to breathe diaphragmatically; gradually it should again become a natural function.

The Most Authoritative Guide to Meditation

Around 500 B.C., the Indian sage, Patanjali, wrote a treatise on life, which consisted of 196 brief statements, called *sutras*. In this classic text are profound metaphysical concepts condensed to their seed form. They describe the whole process we call life, why we suffer and how to return to and live from the blissful and natural state of our Real Self. This great work pierces the veil of illusion and gives a peek into Reality.

Patanjali was not the originator of the content of this treatise. In it he merely sums up the total knowledge of the sages, yogis and meditators. It provides a summary of the nature of life, and how to attain cosmic consciousness.

Patanjali explains that it is thought waves that prevent us from living in harmony with our true nature or Real Self. We identify with our thought waves and we live in this False Self, which we refer to as the ego. When the mind is still, the Real Self, which is our higher consciousness, comes to the forefront. This is a gradual process which takes place over many years of practice and application.

Presented below are a few selected sutras from Patanjali's work, to show how, with brilliant economy and intellect, he explains the meditator's view on life and how to achieve the blissful state of enlightenment. The work is aptly called *The Yoga Sutras* meaning "the knowledge of union".

Sutra 2

Yoga is the inhibition of the modifications of the mind.

Modifications refer to the different types of thought waves, or anything that disturbs the stillness of the mind.

Sutra 3
Then the Seer is established in his own essential nature.

When there are no thought waves, the Seer attains self-realisation and starts living in harmony with his real and natural self.

Sutra 4
In other states there is assimilation of the Seer with the modifications of the mind.

When we are not living according to our true nature, we identify ourselves with our thoughts, but since our thoughts are largely conditioned by our past circumstances, they are not the real us.

The Last Sutra

This sutra states that the final stage of meditation produces enlightenment, and this occurs when we are living according to our real nature, which is pure consciousness.

Patanjali does not recommend the need to suppress our thoughts. Trying to still the mind forcibly, never works and in fact creates greater problems. All the seers agree that there are only two ways to reduce thought waves. One is to observe your thoughts passively by detaching yourself from them. The other is through meditation (focusing or concentrating the mind.)

Prayer is a Powerful Medicine

A well-known study by Randolph Byrd made headlines a couple of years ago.

Byrd, a cardiologist at San Francisco General Hospital, decided to do a study on the efficacy of prayer. He took five hundred patients who had been admitted to the coronary intensive care unit, either for the treatment of heart attack or for ruling out heart attack, and he had them randomly assigned to a 'prayed - for' and a 'not - prayed - for' group.

It was the pinnacle of controlled scientific research — a randomised double blind study. None of the staff knew who was in which group, so they could not preferentially give care to one group and not the other, and the subjects were chosen at a random, so factors like sex, age, health, and demographics would balance out. Then he farmed out their names to prayer groups of various denominations around the country.

When they broke the code at the end of the study, they found that indeed the 'prayed - for' patients did significantly better on a number of measures. They got fewer infections, needed fewer antibiotics, got out of the hospital sooner. No one in the 'prayed - for' group needed a respirator, whereas sixteen or seventeen of the others did.

The differences were so significant that if prayer had been a drug, there would have been a run on the market for it. One well-known debunker of similar studies could find absolutely nothing wrong with this experiment. "Now I can truly say," he wrote, "that physicians should take out their pads and write prescriptions for prayer."

There is no way to explain these results in terms of a brain generating consciousness in the body. The only way to explain it is that somehow, the thoughts of one person can affect another person at a distance.

Two Powerful Techniques to Stop Worrying Right Now

First, when you start to think of the future and are on the brink of anxiety, just say to yourself, "we'll see". Two small words, but they are powerful and can prevent a lot of worry. You do not know what is going to happen tomorrow or further down in life, so why worry about what might or might not happen.

We worry because it is a habit, and the best way to break the habit is to replace worrying thoughts with the positive expression, "we'll see".

The reason why this technique works so well is because the vast majority of our worries never eventuate. That is a fact. Even though they are a figment of our imagination, they cause a lot of distress, accompanied with health problems and premature ageing. Since, in general, worries do not manifest themselves, it is pointless to worry.

By saying, "we'll see" every time you think of some possible future event, the mind will eventually give up worrying, since it has learned not to project itself into the future.

The other way this technique works is based on the fact that whatever we think about, we tend to attract. In other words, what we fear, we tend to attract. This is especially so, if we keep worrying about the same thing. This principle feeds on repetition. But by replacing a worry with "we'll see", we are no longer giving power to that worry; nor are we encouraging that worry in any way.

Another good expression to replace worry is "forget results". If you are in business and are worrying about how business will go this week, replace that worry with the thought, "forget results".

Application of efforts is the cause of success. For example, if you are working on a project and are worried about the results, you are not applying the hundred per cent concentration that the project deserves. Worries make you omit things and commit mistakes.

Concentrate on what you are doing. If you do the right things and put in your best, then the results will take care of themselves.

This expression gives us great relief, since we can now focus on the application of efforts, and stop wasting time worrying about the results.

The Art of Letting Go!

Two monks came to a shallow river and were about to cross when they noticed a young woman. She explained to them that she was too scared to walk across the river. One of the monks said, "Don't worry, I'll take you across". He picked her up in his arms and carried her across.

After the monks had continued their journey for some time, the other monk said, "You shouldn't have taken that young lady in your arms across the river; you know we are forbidden contact with women."

The monk replied, "I let go of that woman after crossing the river bank; you're still carrying her".

This story further emphasises the point that once you have taken a decision and acted on it, there is no point in finding faults with it later. So stop brooding on it and carry on with life.

From Stress to Strength

Tips for Stress reduction

Many changes in life often lead to an accumulation of stress. Here is a list of 25 simple, common-sense strategies for transforming mental, physical and emotional tension into energy that is creative and effective.

- Take time to be alone on a regular basis, listen to your heart, check your intentions, re-evaluate your goals and your activities.

- Simplify your life! Start eliminating the trivial things. Do not think too much about the minor things in life.

- Take deep, slow breaths frequently, especially while on the phone, or in the car, or waiting for something or someone. Use every opportunity to relax and revitalize yourself.

- Each day, plan to do something that brings you joy, something that you love to do, something just for yourself.

- When you are concerned about something, talk it over with someone you trust, or write down your feelings.

- Say 'No' in a firm but kind way when asked to do something you really do not want to do.

- Exercise regularly! Stretching your body releases tension.

- Remember, it takes less energy to get an unpleasant task done "right then" than to worry about it all day.

- Take time to be with nature, people you like, and children. Even in the city, noticing the seasonal changes or watching people's faces can be a good harmoniser.

- Consciously practise doing one thing at a time, keeping your mind focused on the present. Do whatever you are doing slowly, more intentionally, and with more awareness and respect.

- Choose not to waste your precious present life being guilty about the past or being concerned for the future.

- Learn a variety of relaxation techniques and practise at least one, regularly.

- When you find yourself angry in situations, ask yourself, "What can I learn from this?" Anyone or anything that makes you angry is showing you how you let yourself be controlled by your expectations of how someone or something should be. When you accept yourself, others, and the various situations for what they are, you become more effective in influencing them to change according to your wishes.

- Become more aware of the demands you place on yourself, your environment, and on others — to be different from how they are at any moment. Demands are tremendous sources of stress; therefore, be more reasonable in your demands and reduce stress.

- If you have a hectic schedule, prioritise your activities and do the most important ones first.

- Take frequent breaks to relax.

- Organize your life in such a manner as to include time for fun and spontaneity. Set a realistic schedule, allowing some transition time between activities. Eliminate unnecessary commitments.

- Laugh, smile, stop worrying and be more happy.

- Learn to delegate responsibility.

- Monitor your intake of sugar, salt, caffeine, and alcohol.

- Create and maintain a personal support system — people with whom you can be "vulnerable".

- Be more kind to yourself and to others.

- Welcome change as an opportunity and a challenge to learn and grow.

- Watch the clouds or the waves on water. Listen to music or to the sounds around you. Notice the silence between the sounds and space between the objects.

- In this journey of life, remember to stop and smell the flowers!

The Basis and Benefits of Mantra Healing

A Mantra is a syllable, a word or a set of words of immense spiritual power, handed down in a spiritual tradition for many years.

The repetition of a Mantra is a means of improving the powers of concentration. There are Indian spiritual masters who maintain that the meaning and the content of the Mantra do not necessarily have to be understood by the aspirant in order to bring about the desired effect.

That the practice of Mantra alone is sufficient to achieve the spiritual awakening which is its purpose.

Certainly, the use of the Mantra purifies the subconscious. Even if it is repeated mechanically, some purification will take place. However, each mantra is devotional by nature and has the Divine as its form and essence. With concentration on the meaning of the mantra, the attainment of the ultimate goal is surer and quicker.

The benefits of Mantra practice depend on you as an individual — on where you start, where you stand now, what your past life has been, and the intensity and degree of longing in your desire. When you chant a Mantra your whole being changes for the better.

One of the results that comes quickly with the practice of Mantra, is, control of the breath — the means by which we can develop the ability to control the emotions. While chanting, we give all our emotions to the Mantra, to the deity of the Mantra, and ask that deity to help us gain control. In this way we find a safe release for negative feelings. Rather than throwing them on someone else, we offer them back to their source. Continued chanting will lead to greater awareness and the replacing of negative feelings with positive affirmations.

Mantra practice subdues turbulent emotions and thereby calms the turbulent mind. In yogic terms there is a difference between emotions and feelings — a purified emotion becomes a true feeling. Mantra Yoga gives us an opportunity to know the emotions: what they are, where they come from, and what their proper place is in our lives. Through Mantra Yoga we can learn to deal with emotions properly, to control and refine them, and to encourage the harmonious development of all the aspects of human potential.

As the Mantra is put into the subconscious, the mind is purified to an extent which we would be incapable of, without this aid. Slowly the ego is overpowered by the Higher Self. It is like pouring milk into a cup of black coffee until, little by little, the coffee is replaced by pure milk. As it purifies the mind, the Mantra is also a great protection from fear.

When emotions are purified they develop into love, which is an important step in the awakening of further levels of consciousness, and thereafter, the influences of the Mantra become very subtle. Feelings, which have been purified, bring us into the presence of the Divine, and from the Divine we feel a sense of protection. The Mantra is like a shield against all that is negative and disturbing.

The voice can become an instrument for expressing and controlling the emotions. At times your chanting may be caressing, gentle, intense, full of longing or surrender. If you chant softly, you may observe that your emotions become more gentle. They will become refined through the chanting and change into true feelings which are expressed by the heart. At other times your voice may be strong and powerful, as you put into it all your anger and disappointment, your requests and demands. Honestly express to God what you feel, even your anger and impatience towards the Divine for not bringing you sooner to the Light. However, you must also learn to control your emotions, or your practice will become an emotional self-indulgence.

When you find that your emotions are beyond control, you may give them back to the Divine. You may address the Divine at a very personal level, saying, "Why did you give me all these emotions? Why did you not give me the strength and insight to handle them? I want you to come here now and do something about it." This may not seem like a form of prayer, but it is. It is the recognition of the need for help, and the willingness to ask God for that help, and that is humility.

In chanting out the emotions, from the ugliest to the most exalted, and giving them back to the One who gave them to you in the first place, you learn to accept both parts of yourself, the good and the bad, and to transcend the pairs of opposites, from which you are trying to free yourself. On the spiritual path, by channelling the emotions towards God, you find that the Divine accepts your struggle, aids and sustains you in your search for the Ultimate.

Emotions in themselves are not bad, but when running wild, they can be extremely damaging. Even love, when not shared or given freely and generously, becomes self-love, which turns back destructively on the individual. When emotions are directed, they are a source of strength for great achievements. Through the power of emotions, men and women have overcome their limitations and attained a higher purpose in life. Emotions, channelled through a Mantra towards the Divine, can take you closest to God.

When chanting a Mantra, the emotions express themselves in the breath and the voice. Every time the breath is uneven it means that the emotions are involved and we are out of balance. As long as the emotions are running high, this imbalance exists, but gradually they subside and we begin to experience the equilibrium that is our goal.

Chanting helps us to achieve this stillness by bringing the breath and the emotions under control. In these moments of complete stillness of the mind, indescribable bliss is experienced. By repeated practice, it becomes possible to hold on to the contact made with our innermost being.

As the Mantras are chanted, moods are brought under control and awareness in the here and now grows. Attention, and therefore energy, is withdrawn from the old thought patterns which, like tapes on a tape recorder, were playing over and over. These mental background noises keep us tied to the past and to the future, to fearful imaginings and senseless fantasies, which cause our self-created sufferings.

The ability to concentrate, to achieve single-pointedness, and the overcoming of self-will, go hand-in-hand. Through the practice of Mantra and Japa Yoga, you will find yourself in direct confrontation with the lower self, the ego or the mind. You will become aware of those aspects of your personality that have been in control and have ruled your life. Now, the Higher Self begins to take possession.

To overcome the ego, one must practise surrender. One must be able to surrender to the Mantra itself and to the energy of the Mantra. Learning to surrender to the Mantra and to the energy of the Mantra, puts in motion the process of purification of the self, by eliminating selfishness, self-glorification, self-justification, and self-gratification.

If you go to bed at night and fall asleep with the Mantra, it will probably stay with you and you will wake up with it. You will not have nightmares, because the generative power of the Mantra dissolves problems and removes the pressures that come from self-importance and self-will.

Through the use of Mantra a greater sensitivity, a refinement of the senses, comes about, which may eventually bring you to the point where you can see with the inner eye and hear with the inner ear. When the inner ear is developed, the music of the spheres may be heard — music of such exquisite beauty as no instrument, no human voice, is able to produce. The Cosmic *Om* might be heard. The impact and effects of such experiences will bring an intense desire to change for the better.

Mantra is not a magic pill; rather it is like a steady stream of water which gradually wears down the hardest stone. The immediate results of chanting are an increase in the ability to concentrate, followed gradually by control of the breath and the emotions. Later the emotions will become refined into true feelings. The most important goal in chanting, however, is the Realisation of the Self.

Meditation — Highlights and Tips

- Meditation is a natural, simple, effortless technique for quietening the mind and for revealing the True Self. It results in inner peace and happiness.

- Since the mind is the root cause of stress, failure and unhappiness as well as calmness, success and happiness, it is logical that we should give time and direct our attention to the mind. Meditation has a more powerful and beneficial effect on the mind than any other known activity.

- Meditation is so simple that anyone can do it. It is also very natural; it requires no drugs or equipment and costs nothing.

- Meditation is different from relaxation techniques, since it produces a deeper level of relaxation and unfolds our Higher Consciousness.

- You will feel the beneficial effects right after your first meditation and since the effects are cumulative, you will experience increasing benefits as time goes by.

- Meditation causes you to enjoy everything to a greater extent, including material things, but your happiness no longer depends on these things, since you are anyway happy from within.

Why Should One Meditate?

Scientists like to define meditation as a state of restful alertness in which the mind is relaxed, yet alert. It is often called the meditative state of consciousness, because it is different from our normal waking and sleeping consciousness.

Since the mind is the source of happiness or unhappiness, stress or mental composure, sickness or well-being, failure or success, it is only logical that we should direct our attention to the mind. Even doctors admit that at least seventy per cent of physical diseases are psychosomatic, that is, they originate in the mind. So for every ten people who declare themselves sick, seven suffer from illnesses which originate in the mind, whether triggered by fear, worry, anger, jealousy or any other negative emotion.

Moreover, once we start meditating, we become more peaceful, less reactive and more stable — all these states lead to greater efficiency in our life with less stress or friction.

Anxiety and panic lead to wastage of energy. Tense muscles, overactive nerves and an overactive mind drain our energy reserves. Becoming calm energizes you once again.

Calmness and vitality are complementary. People who are "hyper" may seem energetic but they are actually fuelled by nervous energy. They end up being irritable and mentally exhausted when their nervous energy wears off.

You can feel the beneficial effects of meditation right after the first few sessions. The effects are subtle but cumulative. So, with every passing day you will find yourself a little less stressed and a little more happy.

Is Meditation Taking us Away from the Reality?

The reality is that, all negative feelings — like worry, anxiety, regrets and guilt which cause wastage of energy — are not Reality. It is just that we have become so accustomed to these negative states of mind, that we assume that they make up the real world.

There really is a better and more peaceful way of living. This 'other reality' emerges when our higher consciousness is allowed to shine through, and this is only possible if we are able to quieten the mind through meditation.

All through our lives, we carry with us, two heavy burdens — the thoughts and regrets of the past and the worries and expectations of the future. At each and every moment, these burdens weigh us down. Meditation allows us to see this reality, and to take a rest from following our ingrained and conditioned patterns of behaviour.

Does Meditation Lead to Expansion of Consciousness?

When thought waves are reduced through meditation, the higher consciousness is given a chance to inundate your mind.

We experience glimpses of our higher consciousness at various stages of our lives — moments of utter peacefulness, feelings of bliss. This is the higher consciousness expressing itself, but because our minds live on the thinking level constantly, these moments are rare.

In fact, when your mind is crowded with thoughts, the functioning of your innate intelligence is restricted.

Does Meditation Mean Having No Possessions?

Of course, you can go on liking and owning possessions. But your attitude towards them will be marked by a healthy detachment : They will serve you instead of your serving them. A more serene outlook makes you less disposed to buy things you can ill-afford. It stops you from racing to keep up with your neighbour. Your desires for unnecessary things will also decrease.

When you become less stressed and are living more according to your higher consciousness, you enjoy everything more — including material things. Now consider this — if you do not feel good from within, how can you enjoy the material things outside?

The whole basis of meditation is to make you enjoy life more. The beauty of meditation is that it makes you happy from inside, so you are happy anyway, irrespective of whether you are materialistic or not. Your happiness is not dependent on external factors. So you get not only happiness, but freedom too.

Happiness comes from within, and unless you pay attention to what is within you, you will remain stressed and unhappy, regardless of your economic situation.

Other Titles by Vikas Malkani

A master's secrets of Love, Relationship and Marriage. Both these books are invaluable guides for those seeking real love and fulfilment in their lives and relationships.

Ideal for gifting to your loved ones, the perfect place for these books is by your bedside or in your purse/briefcase for constant reference.

Reflections on God, Love, Life, Fear, Relationships... From the author's personal diaries. These three books contain potent spiritual seeds to bring about quantum leaps in your inner consciousness.

Perfect for self-introspection, these books will grow with you and become as faithful friends providing strength, support and wisdom in times of need.

A book that changes lives, this has been a perennial best-seller. In an entertaining and enlightening manner, the author has woven a story which makes the depth of spiritual wisdom available in the simplest of language.

One identifies with the characters in the book, who seem to live lives similar to ours.

The book is full of wisdom stories and brings across the secrets of the universe in an easy, relaxed manner. One actually begins to wonder why such knowledge was never presented so simply and beautifully ever before.

This book brings alive the author's message: "Happiness must not be a mere concept which should be discussed and debated, but a true value that should be apparent in our lives and interactions with people."
Destined to be a classic.